Lemons or Lemonade?

An Anger Workbook for Teens

Jane F. Gilgun, PhD, LICSW

Createspace

ALSO BY JANE GILGUN

Children's Books

Busjacked!
Emma and her Forever Person
Five Little Cygnets Cross the Bundoran Road
Patrick and the Magic Mountain
The King's Toast
The Little Pig Who Didn't go to Market
The Picking Flower Garden
Turtle Night at Playa Grande
Will the Soccer Star

Books

Child Sexual Abuse: From Harsh Realities to Hope
Children with Serious Conduct Issues
I Want to Show You: Poems
The NEATS: A Child & Family Assessment

Manuals

Lemons or Lemonade? An Anger Workbook for Kids
Lemons or Lemonade? A Manual for Professionals and Parents of Kids
Lemons or Lemonade? A Manual for Professionals and Parents of Teens
Readiness to Adopt Children with Special Needs

Jane Gilgun is a professor and writer. She has many articles and assessment tool available on social media websites such as scribd.com, Amazon Kindle, and smashwords.com.

Teens and Anger

Teenagers get angry. Anger is normal and natural. Teens require the guidance of adults to learn how to express their anger. That is the purpose of this workbook: to help teens learn how to express their anger appropriately. By appropriately, I mean in ways that foster open communication and do not harm others or the self. Parents and teachers will find the ideas and exercises in this book helpful. When teens and teachers find that teens' expressions of anger are too much for them, they may seek the help of professionals. This workbook is made for anger management education for young people 13 and older.

I wrote this workbook and the manual for parents and professionals after years of work with families and young people. I saw over and over how angry and hurt many young people are. Some anger issues are fairly easy to work with. Youth with easy to work with issues may be doing what they have seen others do. Helping young people to express anger appropriately involves direct instruction from adults as well as long-term relationships with adults who handle their own anger appropriately. This is uncomplicated, simple anger that responds to gentle, yet firm instruction that spells out what is acceptable behavior and what is not.

For some young people, anger is the tip of an iceberg. This is complex anger. Fear, hurt, frustration, unworthiness, a sense of being bad, and a desire to be on top could be linked to expressions of anger. For teens with complex anger, some pretty bad things have happened, like abuse and neglect, witnessing violence against their mothers, and other traumas such as war, car accidents, and forced migration. Anger is an expectable response to such adversities. Teens' anger in these circumstances are expressions of many emotions and not only anger. They often find that how they express their anger helps them feel better, but often these are temporary solutions that hurt the teens and sometimes hurt other people. Reactions such fighting, overeating, cutting, fighting, lying, stealing, and running away are examples. Some of the emotions that underlie anger and its expression can be hurt, humiliation, frustration, pride, and isolation. Many young people discover that they feel better when they bully others, torment animals, eat a lot, masturbate, or cut themselves. Even young teens smoke pot and drink alcohol to sooth themselves.

Parents and teachers may not know how to help young people who have complex anger. Some parents have experienced traumas similar to their teen's. If they are overwhelmed by their own issues, they are unable to comfort their teen and to teach and show their teen how to cope. Even if they deal fairly well with their own issues, they may not know how to guide their teens to more appropriate expression of anger.

Many teens think they are supposed to be aggressive when they are angry. They've learned this through watching how their parents and other adults express their anger. Many teens think they are supposed to shout at others and hit others when they are angry. They've seen their parents and other adults do this. Such behaviors seem normal and natural. If these young people have experienced trauma, anger management is part of a program that teens and their parents require to deal with trauma and their responses to trauma.

Here's an example. A 13 year-old boy didn't start trouble but, when he felt provoked, he attacked. The teachers said he was a good kid who wanted to do well in school, but he couldn't learn to read. He was frustrated about that. The school social worker knew the boy well. He lived with a mother who drank to drunkenness every day. She had a younger son whom the boy thought she favored. Whenever she felt anger toward her older son, she beat him. He never hit her back. She yelled at him, made fun of the size of his penis, and neglected him. One night, he phoned the police for help when his mother beat him. They arrived right away and took him to the hospital where he stayed overnight. He told the nurses he did not want to go back home. He wanted foster care. His mother said she did not want him home. After two nights in a shelter, child protection returned him to his mother's house. Three days later, she beat him again. He did not call the police. He left the house and walked the streets all night smoking weed.

This young person would benefit from the exercises in this workbook that is part of a program that includes family and trauma-focused therapy and education about trauma, emotions, and relationships. He is a good candidate for tutoring and vocational training where reading skills are not essential. His mother would be difficult to engage in treatment. As long as she is aggressive toward him and neglects him, this boy will continue to have difficulties. If young people are to learn to manage their emotions and behaviors and live happy lives, their parents must change their own behaviors and show them how to live well.

Part of learning to cope with trauma related to parental aggression is developing skills to cope with powerful emotions related to rejection and fear. Using this workbook when family issues go unaddressed may be helpful but would be most effective in a program of treatment that includes trauma-focused family therapy and parental change.

Some young people value gang membership. Gangs offer belonging and a sense of family that all persons want. Unfortunately, gangs sometimes get what they want through aggression and violence. Guiding gang members away from violence involves acknowledging the importance of being part of a group while showing alternatives to violence. In other words, what young people want from gangs may be what most people want: respect, a sense of belonging, and a purpose in life.

Acknowledging the sources of teens' discontent, identifying how teens currently deal with their discontent, and guiding them toward attaining their goals without hurting themselves or others are goals of this workbook.

Young people can learn to express their anger in ways that foster communication and that do not harm themselves or others. This workbook guides teen's anger toward constructive expressions that turn the lemons of adversity into lemonade.

Jane F. Gilgun, PhD, LICSW
Minneapolis, Minnesota, USA
August 30, 2012

Using this Workbook

For Teens

Anger is an important emotion. It fosters communication and builds relationships when expressed appropriately. What counts is what you do when you are angry. The exercises in this workbook will show you how to express anger so that you will feel better and you will not hurt others or yourself. Many of the things in this workbook will help you build skills that you can use to make a good future for yourself and your family and friends.

For Professionals

For maximum benefits, professionals would use this workbook in the course of work with youth and their families. Doing the exercises in groups with youth and then having the youth show their parents what they have done in the group that day is an effective approach. Work with individual youth would also be effective, especially when parents are involved. If parents or other adults who have a long-term presence in youth's lives are unavailable, teens will still benefit from this workbook, but some of the potential gains may be offset by lack of parental support.

Allow each youth to go through the notebook at her and his own pace. Encourage youth to share their thinking and any material they develop. Some youth may want to act out scenarios they discuss. Some young people may want to hold back a bit from sharing. Please respect their wishes. A ground rule that often works is "You don't have to share anything they do not want to share." Also let them know about your duty to report and your duty to warn. Give them examples of the kinds of behaviors you are required to report. Also, let them know they have a 5th amendment right not to incriminate themselves and so they do not have to give details of any unlawful behaviors.

For Parents

Parents could this material with their teenagers and with younger children as well, when the anger issues are simple and not complex. In addition, parents must know how to manage their own anger constructively. When children have complex anger—that is, anger that is connected to hurt, sadness, frustration, self-hatred, and worthlessness—then parents and young people require professional guidance.

Some youth may not want to talk to you about their anger. Tell them you will be ready when they are and that you will stand by them no matter what. If they have broken the law, they have to take the consequences, but you will be there for them while wanting them to be accountable. Overall, be sure to provide them with love and guidance while at the same time setting firm and consistent limits.

Parents who are raising children who have issues with expressions of anger—such as aggression, depression, and self harmful behaviors—can use support from professionals and other parents whose children have similar issues. Seek that support.

Contents

1. Reasons to be Angry ... 1
2. Do You Deserve it? ... 4
3. Do Other Teens Deserve it? ... 5
4. People I Respect ... 7
5. Respect ... 8
6. What Do You Do When You are Angry? ... 9
7. Anger is Like a Sour Lemon Taste ... 11
8. Doing Things to Feel Better ... 12
9. Feeling Better...for a Little While ... 13
10. The Endless Circle ... 14
11. Making Lemonade ... 15
12. Adults I Can Talk to ... 23
13. Lemons or Lemonade? ... 24
14. Your Turn ... 25
15. The Making Lemonade Checklist ... 26

Doing Something Really Well ... 27

Further Reading ... 28

About the Author ... 29

Reasons to be Angry

Some teens have lots of reasons to be angry. **Bad things happen to good kids.** Put a check mark in front of the things that have happened to you. Some of these things might not be happening now, but check them if they have ever happened, *even once.*

___ Other people don't like you.
___ Other people make fun of you.
___ Other people don't respect you.
___ Things that go wrong are your fault.
___ You don't live with your family.
___ You are ashamed of where you live
___ You don't feel like you belong.
___ You feel like no one cares what you think.
___ Other people pick on you.
___ Your mother gets high on drugs.
___ Your father gets high on drugs.
___ Your mother gets drunk.
___ Your father gets drunk.
___ You are ashamed of your mother.
___ You are ashamed of your father.
___ You saw someone get hurt.
___ You don't feel safe at home.
___ You don't feel safe at school.
___ You don't feel safe in your neighborhood.

___ Someone you love doesn't love you.

___ You're not welcome in some neighborhoods.

___ Your father hits your mother or someone else.

___ Your mother hits your father or someone else.

___ Your brother or sister makes fun of you.

___ Someone makes you do sexual things.

___ You feel bad about something you did.

___ You can't read like the other teens.

___ You can't do math like the other teens.

___ You're not good in sports.

___ You get yelled at.

___ Someone hits you or beats you up.

___ Someone you loved died.

___ Other people steal your things.

___ You miss friends when you move.

___ A pet died.

___ You move a lot.

___ You think you're ugly.

___ You don't have any friends.

___ You feel unwanted.

How many did you check? _____

Do the things you checked make you angry?	*Yes*	*No*
Do the things you checked make you sad?	*Yes*	*No*
Do the things you checked make you angry and sad?	*Yes*	*No*

Feeling Angry & Sad

Teens feel angry about these things. They feel sad, too. Sometimes they have a burning feeling inside. Sometimes they go from feeling angry to feeling sad to having that burning feeling. Right now you may be feeling sad or angry or both. You might have that burning feeling inside, too. **This is not much fun**.

You can use this space for anything you want. Have things happened to you that are on this list? Not on this list? You can write about them. You can draw a picture about them, or you can look around to see if there is an adult you can talk to.

My Space

Do You Deserve it?

Teens sometimes believe they did something to deserve bad things. Some teens think they are bad when other people treat them bad. Here are things that some teens think. Circle yes or no to the following questions.

• *I do bad things.*	Yes No
• *I think I'm bad.*	Yes No
• *Other people tell me I'm bad.*	Yes No
• *Sometimes I think I am bad but no one has told me I am bad.*	Yes No
• *I like being bad.*	Yes No
• *Bad things happen to me because I'm a bad kid.*	Yes No
• *If I had been a better kid, bad things would not have happened*	Yes No

**If you think you are bad…. even sometimes,
what is that like?**

Use the space below to draw a picture or write about what it's like to think you are bad. If you think it's good to be bad, you could draw a picture about that or write something. You can also leave this space blank.

Do Other Kids Deserve it?

Teens sometimes believe that some people deserve to be treated bad. Circle yes or no to the following questions.

- *Some teens deserve to be beaten up.*   Yes   No
- *Some kinds deserve to be teased.*   Yes   No
- *I can take things from others teens if I want them.*   Yes   No
- *It's okay to tease teens I don't like.*   Yes   No
- *It's okay to tease teens who are ugly.*   Yes   No
- *It's okay to do mean things to other teens if I enjoy it.*   Yes   No
- *It's okay to trick other teens into doing things.*   Yes   No
- *It's okay to lie to get other teens to do things.*   Yes   No
- *It's okay to force other teens to do things.*   Yes   No
- *Teens deserve it when other people are mean to them.*   Yes   No
- *It's okay to make other teens cry if I think they are bad.*   Yes   No

What other things do teens do that make others feel bad or sad? Write them below.

What I Think

Teens have opinions about good and bad things in their lives. Check the items below that you agree with.

___Bad things can happen to good kids.

___Good kids sometimes do bad things.

___If someone does bad things to me, I want them to stop.

___It is wrong to do bad things to other people.

___It takes courage to talk to someone about what's bothering you.

What I Think

You probably have other opinions about these things. Use the space below to express them. Write, draw, use watercolor, pastels, or write a poem. Do what you want with this blank page.

My Space

People I Respect

You probably respect some people. Think of who they are. Then answer the following questions. If you don't know anyone you respect, then skip to the next page.

Who are the people you respect? _____

_____

How do the people you respect treat other people? _____

_____

How do they treat you? _____

_____

What do these people do when they are disrespected? _____

_____

What do these people respect about you? _____

_____

What do you do to get their respect? _____

_____

How do you know these people respect you? _____

_____

Respect

Teens want respect. It's one of the best feelings in the world. Disrespect is a big reason why teens get angry. Circle yes, no, or maybe to the following statements.

Respect means recognition for the thing you can do.	Yes	No	Maybe
Most teens get angry when they don't feel respected.	Yes	No	Maybe
Most teens feel hurt when they don't get respect.	Yes	No	Maybe
Respect means having friend who admire me.	Yes	No	Maybe
It's lame to want respect.	Yes	No	Maybe
Everyone wants respect.	Yes	No	Maybe
When I'm not respected, I get mad.	Yes	No	Maybe
I get back at people who don't respect me.	Yes	No	Maybe
The bigger hit of drugs I take, the more others respect me.	Yes	No	Maybe
When I'm disrespected, I feel like I'm no good.	Yes	No	Maybe
Teens who have nice clothes and fancy cars get respect.	Yes	No	Maybe
I have to have money to get respect.	Yes	No	Maybe
Having a kid or two gets me respect.	Yes	No	Maybe
Making people afraid of me gets me respect.	Yes	No	Maybe
Real men get respect.	Yes	No	Maybe
People won't respect me if I don't have nice clothes, a car, & cash.	Yes	No	Maybe
Being good at sex gets respect.	Yes	No	Maybe
Having a baby daddy or a sugar mamma gets me respect.	Yes	No	Maybe
Not taking nothing from nobody gets me respect.	Yes	No	Maybe
Other things are more important than respect.	Yes	No	Maybe
Self-respect is not important.	Yes	No	Maybe

What Do You Do When You are Angry?

What do you do when you are angry? Here are some things teens do. Put a check mark beside the things you do when you are angry or sad.

___You think no one respects you.
___You beat someone up.
___You don't talk.
___You pretend everything is okay.
___You think about something that makes you happy.
___You pick on other teens.
___You talk to someone.
___You listen to music.
___You do yoga.
___You hurt animals.
___You annoy other people.
___You destroy other people's property.
___You think about hurting other people.
___You do something nice for someone else.
___You set fires.
___You cut yourself.
___You steal.
___You sniff glue, paint, gasoline, smoke dope, take drugs, or drink alcohol.
___You read a book.
___You feel you are watching yourself from far away.
___You draw pictures about things that make you angry.

___You think about getting back at the person who made you angry.

___You think about running away.

___You run away.

___You work hard at something, like school work.

___You do sexual things to yourself.

___You do sexual things to others.

___You eat a lot of food.

___You throw up after you eat a lot of food.

___You cut yourself.

___You do things to make other people mad at you.

___You refuse to do what other people tell you to do, like teachers who want you to do your homework or parents who want you to come in at night.

___You tell jokes.

___ You talk big.

___You write poetry.

___ I talk trash about people behind their backs.

___Something else? What? _____

How many items did you check? _____
How many of these things don't hurt anyone else or yourself? _____
How many make things better? _____

There's nothing wrong with being upset and angry. You have reasons to be angry if you feel disrespected, if someone beats you up or talks trash to you, if your parents ignore you, if someone yells at you, makes fun of you, if you feel you don't belong anywhere, if you have been sexually abused, and if no one cares what you want. What's important is what you do when you are angry and upset.

Anger is Like a Sour Lemon Taste

For lots of teens, anger is like a sour lemon taste in your mouth. If you don't do something that helps it go away, anger can grow. It can burn. When you are angry, you can do things that hurt yourself or others. First, we'll talk about what anger can feel like. Then we'll talk about how you can deal with your anger so you don't hurt other people or yourself. Anger is normal and natural. It's what you do with it that counts.

For some teens,

- Anger can be sour. It can hurt. It can make you feel helpless. It can make you feel desperate.

- Anger can become like a great big lemon growing inside you. It gets so huge you feel as if you are going to explode.

- It's like someone stuffs a lemon in your mouth and the seeds go up your nose.

- It's like someone straps a huge basket of lemons on your back and you feel as if your back is going to break. You do everything you can to get that heavy burden off your back.

- It's like you're on fire inside.

- Anger can mean you're a bad kid. You may think other people are laughing at you or don't care about you.

- When you're angry, you may think about getting back at other people. This is called revenge.

Doing Things to Make Yourself Feel Better

Anger doesn't feel very good. It's natural to want to do something to feel better. Some of these things teens do help the anger go away. Some of these things make the anger grow.

Complete the sentences below.

When I'm angry, I want to

When I'm angry, I think about

When I'm angry, I think I'm a

When I'm angry, I feel like

Feeling Better... for a Little While

Teens do lots of things to make themselves feel better when they are angry. Sometimes what teens do makes things better. Sometimes what they do makes things worse. What makes things worse is to hurt other people or yourself. What teens did to feel better end up making them feel worse.

Teens may pick on other teens, steal, destroy property, fight with other teens, run away, set fires, drink, use drugs, do sexual things, eat too much, and cut themselves. And you know what? Teens do feel better when they do these things...for a little while. Some teens feel terrific when they do these things...for a little while.

Good Feelings that Turn Bad

These good feelings don't last. In a little while, you start feeling bad again. Sometimes you are ashamed of what you did. Sometimes you feel guilty for what you did. You think about the people you hurt. You're sorry you hurt other people.

Do you ever feel sorry for hurting other people? Yes   No

The Endless Circle

Sometimes, doing something to make yourself feel better does make you feel better at first. Then you start feeling bad about what you did to feel better. Maybe you realize that you hurt someone else or yourself to feel better. It did seem like fun at the time. So, you do something else to make yourself feel better. This something else hurts other people or yourself. Then you feel bad for what you did to make yourself feel better.

Does it make sense to do things that make you feel bad even if they make you feel good at first?   **Yes   No**

It gets to be like a big circle. You feel bad. You want to feel better. You do something to feel better. You feel better at first. Then you realize that you hurt someone else or yourself. You feel bad about that. You want to feel better. You do something to feel better. You feel better at first. Then you feel bad because you hurt someone else or yourself.

It's like the hamster in the wire wheel. Around and around you go. You can't jump off the wire wheel.

You're stuck, like a car stuck in sand. The wheels go around and around, but the car doesn't go anywhere. The sand flies right in your face, and you can't get out of the way.

- *Have you ever felt like a hamster stuck in a wire wheel?*   **Yes   No**
- *Have you ever felt like car stuck in sand?*   **Yes   No**

What do you do when you feel this way?

Making Lemonade

You know what? You can make lemonade out of the lemons of anger. Think of how lemonade tastes on a hot day. Your throat is dry and maybe even a little sore. You bring the glass to your mouth. The flecks of lemon slide over your tongue. The lemonade fills your mouth and slides down your throat. You finish the lemonade and say, "Ah. It tastes so good."

There are things you can do that will make lemonade out of the lemons of anger. These things won't make you feel ashamed or guilty afterward. You won't get in trouble if you do them. You will feel good about yourself. Other people will respect you.

The sour lemon taste of anger will turn to the sweet taste of doing something good. You will feel good about being you, maybe not at first, but after a while you will.

When you do them, you won't hurt other people. You will not hurt yourself. When you do them, the good feelings will last.

You may even feel proud that you did them. You will make lemonade out of the lemons of anger.

Making lemonade out of lemons can be hard work. At first, it might not seem like fun. Keep at it. You will be rewarded!

It's important to want to.

Maybe you don't want to. Think about that.

Making Lemonade

These are some things you can do to feel better, if you want to. Pick the ones you want to do. Some may be better for younger teens, and some may be better for older teens.

The more you do things that make you feel better
and that don't hurt yourself or others, the more you will want to do them.

🙂 **Draw a picture of something that makes you angry.** Use the darkest, angriest colors you can find. Draw monsters, or anything you want that shows how angry you are.

You might even make a story out of pictures. Did things turn out the way you wanted?

🙂 **Draw a picture of something that makes you happy.** Suppose you'd like to ride a horse. Draw a picture of a horse you'd like to ride. Maybe you'd like to ride a flying horse, or a unicorn. You could also draw pictures that tell a story of something you want.

🙂 **Make up a story.** Think up a story about a teen who is angry about something. What made the teen angry? Does anyone else care that the teen is angry? What is the teen feeling? What is the teen thinking? What does the teen want to do? What does the teen do? What happens when the teen takes action? Did the teen talk to anyone about being angry? Write a story as many times as you want. Have the teen have different feelings. Have the teen take different actions. Tell someone else the story if you want to. Make a video of it and post it on YouTube.

☺ **Write a story or poem** about a time you were angry. What happened to make you angry? Did anyone else care? How did you feel? What did you think? Did other people tell you what to do with your anger? What did you do? What happened afterward? Did things turn out the way you wanted them to? Tell the story to someone else if you want to. Maybe you can turn the story or poem into a video and post it on YouTube.

☺ **Write a song about being angry**. It could be about you or about someone else. Say whatever you want. Sing the song to someone else if you want to.

☺ **Learn to play a musical instrument**. Talk to your music teacher about this. Or you may know people who play instruments. Talk to them about how you could learn to play, too.

☺ **Throw a rubber ball against the garage.** Find a rubber ball or tennis balls and throw them as hard as you can against the side of a garage. Make sure there's no one around whom you could hit. Pretend the person you're angry at is there. Yell at the person every time you throw the ball.

Maybe you could tack a target on the wall. See how many times you hit the bull's eye. Pretty soon you will have a good throwing arm for baseball.

Pretty soon you will have a good throwing arm for baseball.

☺ **Run.** Put your running shoes on and run. Run until your chest and legs ache. Run wherever t's okay to run, like sidewalks, along a trail, or a track. Each time your foot hits the ground, say, "I am angry." Say whatever else you want to say, but keep on running. Other teens will think you are practicing for track. Pretty soon you might want to race other teens or try out for the track team.

🙂 **Kick a soccer ball around.**

Take a soccer ball to a field or a park. Kick that soccer ball as hard and as far as you want. Yell as loud as you want about how angry you are. You also might get pretty good at soccer.

🙂 **Dig holes in the backyard.**

Ask your parents where in the back yard you can dig. Using a shovel, dig as many holes as you want. Dig as deep as you want. When you are finished, shovel the dirt back into the holes. Start all over again. You may end up with a freshly dug garden.

🙂 **Plant seeds in your new garden.** Water them. Watch them grow. If you planted flower seeds, give your flowers away. If you planted vegetables, give them to other people, too.

🙂 **Listen to music.** Find music that helps you think of the good things about your life. Some songs are funny. Sometimes they talk about things that are fun to do, like swinging on swings, walking in the woods, playing with other teens. Find that kind of music and get your mind off what is making you angry.

🙂 **Dance to music.** Sometimes dancing to music will help you think about happier things. Move around. Shake your body. Move your hands and feet to the music.

"I'm a good person who sometimes makes mistakes."

☺ **Do yoga or meditate**. Sometimes there are classes for teens on yoga and meditation. These are great ways to relax and feel good.

☺ **Substitute good thoughts for bad.** Whenever you start thinking things like I'm bad" substitute, "I'm a good person who sometimes makes mistakes."

☺ **Ask questions.** If you think you are a bad person because of what someone else has done to you, find someone to talk to about this. Ask them, "Do you think I'm a bad person?" Tell them about the times you think you are a bad person.

☺ **Write in a diary.** A diary is a place for special thoughts. When you're feeling angry, a diary is a good place to express it. You could draw pictures that show how you feel. You could cut out pictures from magazines and paste them in your diary. You could tell stories in pictures or in words or both. Sometimes you might want to write in your diary when you are not angry but are feeling good.

☺ **Read a joke book.** Go to the library and ask the librarian where the teens' joke books are. Read the jokes alone or with a friend, whatever you want. Read them out loud to yourself if you want to. Laugh as loud as you want. You might ask your teacher if you could tell a few jokes to the class. Other books that are not joke books are fun to read, too.

☺ **Have a pretend conversation** with someone who isn't there. It could be your father. Or your mother. Or your favorite aunt who died. Find a picture of that person. If you don't have a picture, you could draw one. Then, pretend the picture is the person. Talk to the picture. Maybe you want to tell the person something that makes you angry. You might want to tell a funny story.

You might want to pretend you are the person you want to talk to. It could be like a game that goes like this. First, move two chairs to face each other. Then, sit in one chair and be yourself. Pretend the other person is in the other chair.

After you have said what you want to say, sit in the other chair. Pretend you are the person you just talked to. Give an answer to whatever you just said as if you are now that person. Then, you can switch back to the other chair and be yourself again and say something. Keep doing this until you want to stop.

🙂 **Find a friend to be with.** Sometimes when you're feeling angry, just being with people you like can help you feel better. Visit them, or call them on the phone. You might tell them about your anger or you could ask them how their day is going.

🙂 **Talk to someone you trust.** Be on the lookout for someone you can talk to. Some teens watch another person for a long time before they decide they can trust this person.

How do you know when you can trust another person? That is a hard question. There are lots of adults who like teen and want to help them out. People you can trust are nice to other people. They don't make fun of other people. You feel good when you are around them.

🙂 **Stand up for yourself.** Sometimes people who are hurting you will stop if you tell them to. You might have to practice with someone else about what to say, someone you trust. You could say to the person who is hurting you, "I don't like what you do. I want you to stop."

If the person doesn't stop, never believe there is something wrong with you. The behavior of the person who is hurting you is wrong. You count. Never believe that you don't count. Find someone to talk to about the person who is hurting you. Don't keep it a secret. You have nothing to be ashamed of. Don't stop looking for adults you can talk to.

🙂 **Do something nice for someone else.** No matter how mad or sad you feel, you can feel better when you do something nice for someone else. How about raking the yard without being asked or text a friend who is home sick from school? Don't text during class! What other nice things can you do for other people?

🙂 **Apologize**. If you have hurt someone, tell this person, "I am sorry I hurt you. I hope you can accept my apology my apology. If you can't, I will understand." Talk to friends and adults about how to apologize. Practice with friends and adults or by yourself in front of a mirror. When you apologize tell the other person exactly what you did that was hurtful.

🙂 **Make restitution**. This means to make up for something you've done that hurt someone else. Maybe you've broken someone else's toy. To make restitution, you would buy a new one. If you broke someone's window, apologize and then make up for it. You could pay for fixing the window or do chores to pay for fixing it.

Learn to do something really well.

🙂 Learn to do something really well. When you are angry, think of something you really like. Then, do it. It doesn't matter what it is as long as it doesn't hurt you or other people. Practice a lot so you can do it really well. Maybe it's jumping rope or shooting hoops. Maybe you like math. Some teens write poetry or like to read. Maybe you like to sing. How about learning to play a musical instrument? You might find other teens who like what you like. Soon you have new friends.

🙂 Say, "I am hurt by what you did."

It's great to tell persons who have hurt you, "I am hurt by what you did." It would be wonderful if these persons say to you they're sorry, that they never meant to hurt you, and that they will do all they can to make restitution.

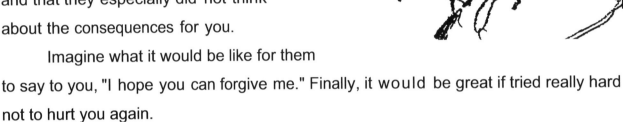

It would be great if they could say they did not think of the consequences and that they especially did not think about the consequences for you.

Imagine what it would be like for them to say to you, "I hope you can forgive me." Finally, it would be great if tried really hard not to hurt you again.

Sometimes this is possible. Teens who have experienced hard times and traumas benefit when people who have hurt them apologize and change their ways. Teens, however, sometimes require preparation for stating their angry feelings and for apologies. This is not simple. Only when teen are ready to state their feelings and to hear an apology should such things happen.

Unfortunately, for many teens, the persons who have hurt them are no longer available. They could have died or for many other reasons are not part of the teen's lives. Perhaps they have a serious mental illness, are chemically dependent, or have moved away.

Some teens risk verbal and physical abuse if they try to talk to persons who have hurt them. Teens require guidance from adults about direct expression of anger in these situations. With guidance from adults, the exercises in this book can help most teens learn to express their anger and other feelings appropriately.

Adults I Can Talk to

Everyone needs someone to talk to. It can be your mother. It can be your father. It can be someone else in the family. Maybe you don't want to talk to anyone in your family. How about a friend's father or mother? Or a friend? What about someone at school? A teacher? A guidance counselor? A social worker? Can you think of anyone who seems to like you? Maybe you can talk to that person.

Who can I talk to? _____

How do you feel when you think about talking to someone about what is going on?

___ afraid
___ hopeful
___ ashamed
___ happy
___ like a sissy or a punk
___ like a sorry ass

What's the worst thing that could happen?_____

What's the best thing that could happen?_____

How do you hope this person will respond? _____

My Space

Lemons or Lemonade?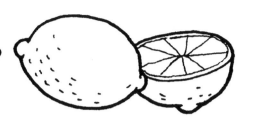

Anger can be as sour and bitter as lemons or you can turn lemons into lemonade. Anger is natural and normal. It becomes sour and bitter when teens don't know how to express their anger. Unexpressed anger can be the tip of an iceberg. Underneath anger there can be guilt, sadness, fear, and feelings of worthlessness. This workbook is for teenagers whose anger has become complicated because they need some help in dealing with their feelings.

Remember, there's nothing wrong with wanting to feel better when you are angry. In fact, it's important to help yourself feel better when you are angry. It is wrong to feel better by hurting others or yourself. Using anger to write a poem, get in shape, or learn something new is the right way to deal with anger. If you do things that make your life better, you will get many of things you want, like respect and self-respect. Doing the right things will also help you make friends and get along with other people.

My Space

Your Turn

What do you think of this workbook? There are no right or wrong answers. State what you think. You can write or draw something here or talk to someone. You can email Jane Gilgun at jgilgun@gmail.com to let her know what you think.

Is there something you do to feel better that is not in this workbook? What? Be specific so I know what you mean.

Is there anything in this workbook you think is lame? What? Be specific so I know what you mean.

Is there anything in the workbook that you already do? If there is, how does that work out for you?

Is there anything you'd like to try? Don't forget. Sometimes you have to keep at it to get the results you want.

The Making Lemonade Checklist

This checklist is for you. You can carry it with you or put it on your bedroom wall. It reminds you that anger is normal and natural. It also reminds you of what to do when you are angry.

☺ Draw an angry picture.
☺ Draw a happy picture.
☺ Write a story, poem, or song
☺ Learn to play a musical instrument
☺ Throw a rubber ball against a wall.
☺ Run.
☺ Kick a soccer ball around.
☺ Dig holes in the backyard.
☺ Plant a garden.
☺ Listen to music.
☺ Dance to music.
☺ Do yoga or meditate.
☺ Substitute good thoughts for bad.
☺ Ask questions.
☺ Think of things that make you happy.
☺ Write in a diary.
☺ Read a joke book.
☺ Have a pretend conversation.
☺ Find a friend to be with.
☺ Talk to someone you trust.
☺ Stand up for yourself.
☺ Do something for someone else.
☺ Apologize.
☺ Make restitution.
☺ Learn to do something really well.
☺ Say "I am hurt by what you did."
☺ What you do _____
☺ _____

Doing Something Really Well

Further Reading

Cairns, Kate (2002). *Attachment, trauma, and resilience: Therapeutic caring for children.* London, UK: British Association for Adoption and Fostering.

Gilgun, Jane F. (2011). Children with mood issues: A case study and a NEATS Assessment. Scribd.com.

Gilgun, Jane F. (2011). Children with serious conduct issues: A case study, a NEATS analysis, and case planning. Kindle & scribd.com.

Gilgun, Jane F. (2011). *The NEATS: A child & family assessment.* Createspace, smashwords, & Kindle.

Gilgun, Jane F. (2012). *The NEATS: A Child & Family Assessment* (3rd ed). Createspace & Kindle.

Gilgun, Jane F. (2011). A NEATS analysis of children with sexual behavior issues. Kindle, iBooks, Nook. A chapter from *The NEATS*.

Green, Ross W., & J. Stuart Ablon (2006). *Treating explosive kids: The collaborative problem-solving approach.* New York: Guilford.

Lieberman, Alicia F. (2004). Traumatic stress and quality of attachment: Reality and internalization in disorders of infant mental health. *Infant Mental Health Journal, 25(4),* 336-351.

Van der Kolk, Bessel A. (2005). Developmental Trauma Disorder: A new, rational diagnosis for children with complex trauma histories. *Psychiatric Annals 35(5), 390-398.*

Van der Kolk, Bessel A. (2005). Developmental Trauma Disorder: A new, rational diagnosis for children with complex trauma histories. *Psychiatric Annals 35(5), 390-398.*

About the Author

Jane F. Gilgun, PhD, LICSW, is a professor, School of Social Work, University of Minnesota, Twin Cities, USA. This is what Jane says about herself: I have worked with families and children for many years. I learned a lot from them, especially how complicated anger can be when people don't learn at young ages how to express it constructively. In the families I has worked with, anger almost always was the tip of an iceberg, covering up many strong negative emotions, such as hurt, sadness, fear, self-hatred, and almost anything bleak you can think of. Often people with serious anger issues have unattended trauma in their backgrounds.

This workbook and the companion manual for parents and professionals are my attempt to foster healthy expression of anger. Anger can open channels of communication and deepen and strengthen relationships. Left unexpressed, anger picks up many other meanings until the mass of hurt, rage, sadness, and fear threatens quality of life.

I worked at a pubic social services agency in Rhode Island for several years and then became a professor. I have many articles and books available on the Internet. Many of them are free or low cost. I also write children's books, books for adults, articles, and poetry that are available on Amazon, Smashwords, and scribd.com for a variety of mobile devices like Kindle, iPad, & Nook. I have many videos on YouTube that include the landscapes in Northwest Ireland, trail riding in Minnesota and elsewhere, horse racing, pig racing, and more.

My interests include my horses, Padron's Elegante (Ellie) and Finn MacCool, who are mother and son, my dog Jazz, gardening, photography, cooking, the arts, hiking, and spending time in County Leitrim and County Sligo, Ireland.

I have a PhD from Syracuse University in child and family studies and other graduate degrees from the University of Chicago in social service administration and from the Catholic University of Louvain in Belgium in family studies and sexuality. I also have a bachelor's and master's degree in English and American poetry from the Catholic University of America and the University of Rhode Island, respectively. I am a professor, School of Social Work, University of Minnesota, Twin Cities, and a licensed independent clinical social worker.

First published in the United States of America in 1998

Copyright © 1998-2012 by Jane Gilgun
jgilgun@gmail.com

The rights of Jane Gilgun to be identified as the author of this work have been asserted by her in accordance with the Copyright Designs
and Patents Act of 1988.

All rights reserved. No part of this publication may be reproduced, stored in retrieval systems, or transmitted in any form or by any means, electronic, mechanical, photocopying, recording, or otherwise, without the prior written permission of the copyright owner, except for brief quotes in reviews, articles, and blogs.

Gilgun, Jane.
Lemons or Lemonade? An Anger Workbook for Teens
revised edition

1. Child development 2. Anger management. 3. Parenting 4. Social services
5. Education 6. Childhood aggression 7. Resilience.

ISBN-13: 978-1479207213
ISBN-10: 1479207217

Createspace

Visit Amazon Kindle, Google Books, iBooks, & other Internet booksellers
to discover other books, articles, and children's stories by Jane Gilgun
that you may enjoy.

Cover design by Therese Graner
Book design by Jane Gilgun

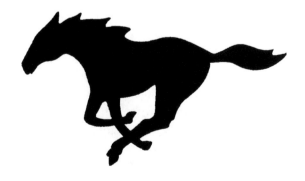

Made in the USA
San Bernardino, CA
11 November 2015